Student Loan Planning

A Borrower's Guide to Understanding and Repaying Student Loan Debt

Ryan H. Law, CFP®, AFC®

ISBN-13: 978-1718079434

DEDICATION

To my wife, Traci, who has always believed in and supported me.

DISCLAIMER

This book is designed to provide accurate information in regard to the subject matter covered at the time of publication. It is published with the understanding that the author is not engaged in rendering legal, accounting, financial, or other professional service. If legal or financial advice or other expert assistance is required, the services of a competent professional should be sought.

CONTENTS

Student Loan Planning
A Borrower's Guide to Understanding and Repaying Student Loan Debt

PREFACE

I sat across the desk from Jake[1], who was almost in tears. He had amassed over $200,000 in private student loan debt to get an unmarketable bachelor's degree from a private university. He was working a minimum-wage job, living at home with his parents, and he had not made a single payment on his student loans, all of which his grandmother had co-signed on. Embarrassed about destroying his grandmother's good credit and trust, he had not spoken to her in almost a year.

As I talked with Jake, I was reminded of a quote by Heber J. Grant, "...if there is any one thing that is grinding and discouraging and disheartening, it is to have debts and obligations that one cannot meet[i]."

I saw this in Jake - he was completely discouraged and disheartened. I could feel his pain and anguish as he faced the future.

"Jake," I said, "in all your years of college did no one - a lender, a parent, your grandmother, a financial aid advisor or academic advisor, sit you down and have a discussion about school, careers, and this debt?"

Struggling to get the words out he said, "No. I wish someone had. I was 18 when I started taking these loans out. I didn't know there were no jobs in the field I was getting a degree in. I didn't understand

---

[1] Name has been changed

that I wouldn't have the money to repay these loans. Repayment seemed like it was years into the future. I had no idea. I should have, but someone taking a minute to explain it to me would have helped me avoid this."

I helped Jake come up with a few strategies, but the reality is there isn't much we can do at that point, especially with private student loans.

While Jake's example is extreme, it illustrates a point: **People don't understand student loans!** Think about it for a minute - there are at least five different federal student loan products (and that doesn't include private loan options); nine different payment plans, some that base your payment off the total amount borrowed and some that base your payment off your income and family size; options for delaying payments; forgiveness programs; multiple loan servicers; consolidation; default provisions and much more. No wonder students and their parents are confused!

Despite federally mandated entrance and exit counseling about student loans, research[ii] shows that the majority of borrowers are confused about their debt and the terms they are borrowing on:

- 64% of students worry about having enough money to pay for school
- 65% misunderstood aspects of their loans, including the repayment terms, the amount of their monthly payment, or the interest rate
- 2/3 of borrowers do not understand the difference between federal and private loans

- 60% of students have more student loan debt than they expected to have
- ⅔ of borrowers are not sure they will be able to pay off their student loans

A student who borrowed $150,000 in student loans reported the following:

"I was never offered information on what my monthly payments would look like. They gave me all sorts of Internet surveys about student loans, but the most they ever really said was I would need to pay them back. They never told me they would completely cripple my ability to make any kind of life for myself."

A few years of borrowing started at about age 18, completely crippling the ability of an individual to live the life they imagined.

Unfortunately, what typically happens in cases like Jake's or this borrower is that they can't make payments, they don't know who to turn to, and they give up. They stop paying and they avoid the non-stop calls from creditors. Most will have their wages garnished. Tax returns will be sent directly to the lender. Faced with massive student loan payments, they can't save for the future, so they face a grim retirement. During all of this the debt continues to grow as it goes into collections, where they face as high as a 25% collection fee and interest piles up.

We can do better than this. We *must* do better than this. Students and their parents should be fully educated on student loans and there should be, at a minimum, annual checkpoints with an actual trained person discussing their debt level, career outlooks, salary projections and repayment of their loans. Students want help, too. In fact, more than ⅔ of students said they would use financial support services if it was offered by their school. Unfortunately, most universities don't have an office like that, so students don't know where to turn.

Because of my job where I counsel students at a University about their personal finances, I decided to become an expert at student loans. I have studied student loans extensively, helped many current and former students understand and set up a plan to repay their student loans, and presented about them at national conferences.

I can tell you, based on my own experience and the many students and graduates I have helped, that paying off your loans and being free of that debt is completely possible.

This book will give you a baseline understanding of student loans. We will review how to minimize student loans, types of loans, repayment plans, delinquency and default, forgiveness programs, and strategies to pay off debt as quickly as possible.

I have structured the topics in a question and answer format. You can quickly find the question you have and find the answer. However, if you have student loans or you are helping someone who has student loans I would encourage you to read the full book in order to get an overall understanding of how student loans work. I intentionally made the book short so it can be read and referenced quickly. I chose not to discuss the history of student loans or how we can fix the problems in the industry. This book is about *your* loans and how you can pay them back as quickly as possible.

I encourage you to visit my website at https://ryanhlaw.com. This is the best way to get the current news and changes regarding student loans.

If you, or someone you know, is struggling with their debt or wants help making a plan to repay their loans, please send them to that same website. I will help them create a plan to get their debt paid back.

Ryan H. Law

1. HOW CAN I KEEP THE COST OF COLLEGE LOW?

There are several strategies you can utilize to minimize student loans. These include:

- Deciding whether or not college is the right path
- Saving for college
- Going to a low-cost school
- Working while going to school
- Selecting a major that has employers seeking for graduates
- Applying for every scholarship you might be qualified for
- Living like a student

Let's explore each of these topics briefly.

Deciding whether or not college is the right path

Do you have to go to college? Do your children have to go to college? The answer is, it depends. I personally believe that for most people, college is a good investment. Without all my years of school I wouldn't have the great job that I have today.

But that doesn't mean that everyone has to go to college. Is a real estate agent going to be a better agent because they have a degree? I don't think so. Unless they want to move into management or open their own agency, they need their real estate license, not necessarily a degree.

Does someone who wants to have a trade such as being a plumber or an electrician need a four-year degree? Maybe, maybe not. It never hurts to learn how to run a business, but one can learn these trades through technical or trade schools and through an apprenticeship.

Only you can decide whether or not college is the right path for you. Talk to your parents and people in the field you are interested in pursuing.

Saving for college

If you have a child or grandchild going to school you should consider opening a state sponsored 529 plan. These plans are tax-advantaged accounts that allow you to save for college, get tax-free growth and tax-free distribution for college expenses. We won't get into details of 529 plans here, but know that this is a great way to save some money in a tax-advantaged account for education[iii].

Going to a low cost school

If you can get into an Ivy League school or small, private university you should go, regardless of the cost, right? Wrong. I work at an open enrollment public university and the students are engaged, learning real world skills and putting their skills into practice with industry professionals. In my program (Personal Financial Planning) we have more job offers than graduates.

I would encourage almost any student to go to a local low-cost school. Community colleges are a great way to get started. From there you can go on to a more elite graduate school, though there is a debate on whether or not having a degree from an elite university will make any difference when it comes to jobs.

College doesn't have to sink you into debt. I see very little value in going to an expensive university unless you are on scholarship.

In addition to attending a low-cost school, be cautious about extra activities such as study abroad. If you can't afford it or it will not get you better job offers, you don't need to do it.

Working while going to school

I hear parents say all the time, "I don't want my son/daughter to have to work. I want them to focus 100% on school." Sorry to break it to you, but no student is 100% focused on school.

I believe that all students should work, at least part-time, while they go to school. Students who work gain experience, learn how to manage their time, and feel some ownership in their education. They also have some cash to help pay for books, food or other education related expenses. Research[iv] shows that students who work ten to fifteen hours a week on campus are more likely to stay in school and have higher academic success than those who do not work or those who work more hours than recommended.

Selecting a major that has employers seeking for graduates

The recommendation to follow your passion and get a degree in something you love can be short-sighted. Just because you love studying 19th century French poetry[2] doesn't mean that someone is going to give you a job. You go to college to get a job. That's it. You need to research majors and careers before you start down the path of "studying what you love." Choose a minor in 19th century French poetry, but don't major in it. Every college has a career center and academic advisors. Talk with them about your interests.

Applying for every scholarship you might possibly be qualified for

There are scholarships for all kinds of people and situations. Some are through a specific department, some with a college, and there are many scholarships through private companies. Far too many scholarships go unfilled each year. If you are a good student or you have a skill, such as an instrument or you play a sport well, you can find a scholarship. High schools guidance counselors can often lead you to scholarship opportunities, but take the initiative and search out other opportunities. However, be very cautious about paying someone to do a scholarship search for you. Be sure they are a reputable company with verifiable results and a good rating with the Better Business Bureau. Many of them will make promises they can't keep.

Be sure to fill out the Free Application for Federal Student Aid (FAFSA) each year, as many scholarships are dependent on that being on file with the school. See Question 2 for more information about the FAFSA.

---

[2] "What a waste of time! — I mean for someone else that would be an incredible waste of time. It's so bold of you to even choose that." (Groundhog Day)

Live like a student

The newest trend in student life is luxury student housing - with granite countertops, stainless steel appliances, rooftop swimming pools, tanning beds - the works. With luxury housing comes luxury prices. College is supposed to be college - where you live like a student in a cinder block building that retains the heat for about 30 seconds. Live on campus or in a low-cost off-campus apartment. Save your money, and the luxuries, for later. Make friends with people who live in the luxury apartments, though, and maybe they will invite you over to use their rooftop pool.

Talk with your child about paying for college

If you are a parent reading this I would encourage you to sit down with your child before they register for college to have a conversation about paying for school. How much, if any, are you willing to pay?

I was fortunate to receive a four-year tuition and fees scholarship, and I knew that my parents were going to pay for the first year of housing, and that was it. I was welcome home anytime where I could eat and do laundry, but as far as day-to-day living expenses, books, and housing beyond year one I was on my own. Because this expectation was clear, I worked hard to earn additional scholarships and joined a program to become a Resident Assistant (RA) in the dorms so that housing would be paid for.

I encourage you to consider each of these options to see how you can keep your college costs as low as possible.

2. WHAT IS FEDERAL STUDENT AID AND HOW DO I GET IT?

Federal student aid includes:

1. Grants, which do not have to be paid back
2. Student Loans, which do need to be paid back
3. Work-study, which is pay for work, typically on-campus.

Federal student aid is received by filling out the Free Application for Federal Student Aid (FAFSA). This needs to be completed each year and includes information such as the income and assets of the parents (or student if they are independent), and which colleges the student is interested in attending.

The FAFSA takes about 20-30 minutes to fill out. You don't need to pay anyone to help you fill out the FAFSA - you can do it yourself or many schools offer free clinics to help individuals fill out the FAFSA. Check with your school's financial aid office to see if your school offers that assistance.

3. WHAT TYPE OF LOANS ARE AVAILABLE?

The types of student loans available include:

- Federal Stafford Loans, which are available in two forms:
  - Direct Subsidized loans
  - Direct Unsubsidized loans
- Perkins Loans
- Direct PLUS loans, which are available in two forms:
  - PLUS loans for parents of undergraduate students
  - PLUS loans for graduate and professional students
- Private student loans

If you have student loans before 2010 you might also have Federal Family Education Loans (FFEL), which were issued by banks, credit unions, and other lending institutions which were guaranteed by the federal government. Since 2010, however, all loans are funded directly by the federal government.

Direct Subsidized loans: These are loans for students with financial need (see Question 4 for more information about need and how that is determined). Interest is paid by the government while a student is in school or other times the loan is in deferment (see Question 23 for more information about deferment). There is a maximum amount of Subsidized loans a student can receive per year (see Question 4 for more information), and since 2012 they are only available to undergraduate students. No payment is due while the student is in school.

Direct Unsubsidized loans: Unsubsidized loans are available for either students who don't have financial need (see Question 4) or as an additional amount for students who need additional funds beyond what they receive in Subsidized loans. No payment is due while the student is in school, but interest does accrue from the day they are disbursed. The borrower can either choose to pay the interest while they are in school or they can let it accrue, and it will be capitalized, or added to the principal balance, at repayment.

Perkins loans: As of the writing of this book the Perkins loan program is ending. It was a smaller, need-based loan program with a fixed interest rate of 5% and a nine-month grace period (compared to a six-month grace period for Direct loans). Loans were disbursed by the school and are repaid to the school instead of a loan servicer. A number of Congressional members support renewing the program, while others recommend it is not renewed in order to simplify the student loan program.

Direct PLUS loans: Parents of undergraduate students and graduate students can take out the total Cost of Attendance (COA) minus other aid received in Federal PLUS loans. For example, if the cost of attendance at a school is $20,000 and a second year student gets $6,500 in federal student aid, his or her parents can take out $13,500 in Parent PLUS loans. See Question 4 for more information about Cost of Attendance.

PLUS loans have a high origination fee - approximately 4.3%. That means if you borrow $10,000 the government is going to keep $430 of it right off the top. They also carry higher interest rates (currently about 7.5%).

PLUS loans are unsubsidized, which means that interest accrues on the loans from the day they are disbursed. Borrowers can pay the interest while they go to school or let it accrue until repayment begins, at which point the interest will be capitalized, or added to the principal balance.

PLUS loans require the borrower to not have an adverse credit history.

Parent PLUS loans: Parent PLUS loans are loans that belong to the parent, not the child. I have seen a number of cases where the parents take out PLUS loans with the expectation that their child will start making payments after school. The child intends to do this, but as they struggle to get started on a job, pay for rent and pay their other debt they are unable to make additional payments. If you are a parent considering taking out a PLUS loan you need to consider whether or not you can make payments on this loan, as it is very likely that you will be the one making payments. Payments on Parent PLUS loans begins immediately after disbursement, but the parent can request a delay until 6 months after the student graduates. It is important to note that Parent PLUS loans cannot be consolidated with other student loans, but they can be consolidated with other Parent PLUS loans.

Parent PLUS loans are discharged if the borrower (parent) passes away or becomes totally and permanently disabled, or if the student for whom the loan was taken out passes away. However, if both parents took the loan out both have to become disabled or die in order for the loan to be discharged.

Graduate PLUS loans: Graduate PLUS loans are available for all graduate and professional students, up to the cost of attendance minus any other financial aid received. No payments are due until six months after the student graduates or drops below half-time enrollment.

Private student loans: A private student loan is a loan made through a bank, credit union, or other lending institution. Typically, students won't qualify for them on their own because there will be a credit check, so parents or grandparents often end up co-signing the loan.

Most private loans have variable interest rates, which look attractive in a low interest rate environment, but can go up dramatically when rates rise or a payment is late. I have seen interest rates as high as 18%.

All private loans are unsubsidized, so payments will need to be made while the student is in school or a borrower can allow interest to accrue.

Because private student loans don't have the same guaranteed protections as federal loans, such as flexible repayment plans, deferment and forbearance, private loans should be a **last resort**, and federal student loans should rarely be paid off with private student loans. See Question 16 for more details about refinancing loans.

A student should keep their total loan amount as low as possible. You should take out loans in the following order:

1. Direct Subsidized loans
2. Perkins loans (if available)
3. Direct Unsubsidized loans
4. PLUS loans
5. Private loans

Summary of student loans:

Loan Type	Who Qualifies	Origination Fee	Interest During Deferment	When Payments Begin
Direct Subsidized	Undergraduates	1.062%	Government pays	6 months*
Perkins	All students	0%	Government pays	9 months*
Direct Unsubsidized	All students	1.062%	Accrues	6 months*
Parent PLUS	Parents of Undergraduates	4.248%	Accrues	Immediately or can be delayed for 6 months*
Graduate PLUS	Graduate and Professional Students	4.248%	Accrues	6 months*
Private Loans	All students	Varies	Accrues	Immediately or can typically be delayed for 6 months*

* After graduation, dropping below half-time status or withdrawal

4. HOW MUCH FINANCIAL AID CAN I GET?

Federal student aid is determined by several factors, including whether the student is dependent or independent, family income and assets, the year in school, enrollment status and the cost of attendance.

A dependent student is anyone who is unmarried, under the age of 24 and has no dependents.

Once a student gets married, has dependents or enters graduate school they are considered independent.

To get federal student aid the student must file the Free Application for Federal Student Aid (FAFSA) each year. Many schools also use the FAFSA to determine scholarships. See Question 2 for more information about the FAFSA.

The FAFSA determines a family's Expected Family Contribution (EFC), which determines the amount a family is expected to pay for school. It doesn't matter if they actually plan to use that amount for college or not. Once a student is independent only their income and assets are utilized rather than their parents. Independent students typically have low EFCs, which qualifies them for more grants and subsidized loans.

Each college or university has to publish a Cost of Attendance (COA) online, which is the cost of attending that college, and includes tuition and fees; books and supplies; room and board; transportation; and personal expenses. They publish these costs for on and off-campus and for in-state and out-of-state students.

A student's need is calculated by taking the Cost of Attendance (COA) and reducing it by the Expected Family Contribution (EFC), or COA – EFC = Need.

DIRECT SUBSIDIZED AND UNSUBSIDIZED LOAN LIMITS

A dependent undergraduate student can get:
- $5,500 first year; $3,500 of which can be subsidized
- $6,500 second year; $4,500 of which can be subsidized
- $7,500 for the third year and beyond; $5,500 of which can be subsidized

An independent undergraduate student can get:
- $9,300 first year; $3,500 of which can be subsidized
- $10,500 second year; $4,500 of which can be subsidized
- $12,500 for the third year and beyond; $5,500 of which can be subsidized

Graduate students:
- $20,500 per year in unsubsidized loans

Medical Students:
- $40,500 per year in unsubsidized loans

Aggregate limit for Direct Subsidized and Unsubsidized loans:
- Dependent undergraduate students:
  o $31,000; $23,000 of which can be subsidized
- Independent undergraduate students:
  o $57,500; $23,000 of which can be subsidized

- Graduate students:
  - $138,500, which includes their undergraduate loans
- Medical students:
  - $224,000, which includes their undergraduate loans

PERKINS LOANS LIMITS

As a reminder, Congress did not extend the Perkins loan program, so no loans are currently being made. I am including the amount in here in case they extend the program.

Undergraduate students:

- $5,500 per year

Graduate students:

- $8,000 per year

Aggregate limit for Perkins Loans:

- Undergraduates: $27,500
- Graduate students: $60,000, which includes their undergraduate Perkins loans

PLUS LOANS LIMITS

There is no maximum amount you can receive in PLUS loans except the Cost of Attendance minus other financial aid received. If the Cost of Attendance is $40,000 and a student receives total financial aid of $20,500, parents of undergraduates or graduate students could borrow up to $19,500 in PLUS loans ($40,000 - $20,500 = $19,500). There is no aggregate maximum.

5. HOW MUCH SHOULD I TAKE OUT IN STUDENT LOAN DEBT?

The previous question asked how much you can take out in student loan debt, but how much you *can* take out in student loans is a very different question from how much you *should* take out in student loans. Some financial planners will tell you to take the most out that you can, after all, it is (relatively) low-interest debt, with payments that can be spread out up to 25 years, and has tax-deductible interest. Many people take this path - take all you can get and worry about repayment later.

I submit to you that this is *very* bad advice. Yes, everything in the previous paragraph is true - the loans are relatively low-interest, payments can be spread out and the interest paid is typically tax deductible. However, there is a dark side to all of those benefits. Student loans are rarely dischargeable in bankruptcy (see Question 22), there is no statute of limitations (how long they can collect on the debt), defaulted loans face severe consequences (see Question 24) and the interest, fees and penalties can swell a borrower's balance well beyond the original balance. **No other types of loans have these types of provisions tied in.**

6. WHAT ARE ADDITIONAL OPTIONS IF I DON'T GET ENOUGH IN FEDERAL STUDENT AID?

If you take out the maximum amount in loans and you still don't have enough to cover your costs you need to consider taking some drastic measures to cut back, including transferring schools or dropping out of school for a time to work and save money.

STUDENT LOAN STORY

Mike Meru[v] is an orthodontist in Utah who went to the most expensive dental school in the nation and financed his education, most of his housing and an expensive vehicle using student loans. When he graduated he had borrowed more than $600,000, and when the accrued interest was added he owed over $725,000. Mike utilized forbearance for a period, during which time he did not make any payments, and additional interest accrued, which brought his total student loan debt loans to more than $1,000,000.

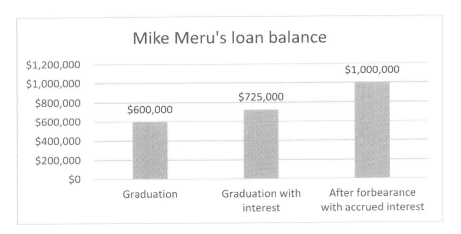

Mike utilizes an income-driven repayment plan, paying 10% of his discretionary income, which makes his payment $1,590 a month. If he utilized the Standard plan his payment would be about $10,500 per month. Because Mike's payment doesn't cover the interest of $3,900 per month, the unpaid interest of $2,300 is added to his loan balance, which means his balance, and the applicable interest, go up each month.

After 25 years of payments Mike will have paid over $1,600,000 and will have approximately $2,000,000 forgiven, for which he will owe roughly $700,000 in taxes. Because Mike's story was published in the Wall Street Journal he has taken a lot of heat for his story. However, in fairness, with Mike paying back $1,600,000 and $700,000 in taxes he will pay about $2,300,000, which is almost four times the original amount he took out in loans.

Mike's story is full of problems and warning signs he should have seen along the way, but the point is that, while Mike's story is extreme, you might be surprised to see how quickly student loans and the associated fees and interest rates can add up.

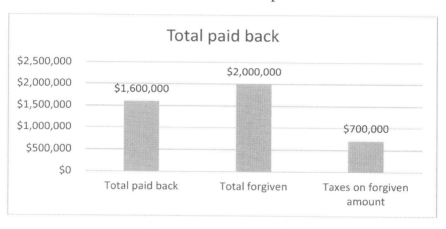

7. HOW DO I ACCESS INFORMATION ABOUT MY STUDENT LOANS?

Student loan data can be accessed through the National Student Loan Data System, or NSLDS. You can access this at NSLDS.ed.gov. You can also call 1-800-4FED-AID. When accessing your loans you can see what type of loan it is, the status of the loan (in deferment, etc.), the total outstanding principal and outstanding interest, the interest rate and who the loan servicer is.

8. WHAT IS THE INTEREST RATE ON STUDENT LOANS?

Interest rates are set each year by Congress. New rates go into effect every July 1. Once the rate is set it will be that rate for the life of the loan. You can check your loan interest rates at www.nslds.ed.gov.

STUDENT LOAN STORY

Alan Collinge started the website Student Loan Justice and wrote a book titled *The Student Loan Scam: The Most Oppressive Debt in U.S. History - and How We Can Fight Back*. In the introduction to his book he shares his story of borrowing $38,000 to get three degrees in aerospace engineering. This would seem to be a fairly low level of debt for a very marketable degree.

Because of accrued interest, however, his debt grew to $50,000 at graduation. His student loan payment equaled about 20% of his take-home pay, but he was getting by. Due to rising rent and utility prices, though, he was late one month and the problems spiraled from there. Every month the payment he made applied to the previous month's payment, which gave him more and more late fees.

Alan freely admits that he made some mistakes along the way, but his loans eventually went into default and are now more than $103,000.

Alan had dreams - have a good job, buy a home, get married and raise a family, but he has given up on most of those dreams.

"Those who have had similar experiences will understand when I say that the debt overwhelmed and paralyzed me. It was completely demoralizing. All the extreme effort, personal sacrifice, late nights studying, and poverty-level subsistence had been endured for the sake of higher education; because of the loans, that education had ended up doing me far more harm than good. I felt like the butt of a very expensive, lifelong joke[vi]."

Alan's story represents a few key points:

1. What seemed like a reasonable amount of debt for a good degree turned out to bury him.

2. A few small mistakes can cause massive problems for a borrower.

3. Student loan debt is causing people to give up on their dreams.

4. Student loan default is very, very bad and should be avoided at almost any cost.

9. CAN I PREPAY MY STUDENT LOANS?

You can prepay federal student loans without a penalty. This is also generally true regarding private student loans, but you will need to check with your loan servicer to be sure.

Payments are always applied to interest, penalties and fees first, and then to the principal balance. If you can pay extra you should generally apply the payment to your highest interest loan. You need to log in to your loan servicer's website, though, and specify the extra payment as a paydown of principal.

If you don't specify that it is a principal paydown your servicer will apply the extra money as a future monthly payment.

Now the more important question is, *"should* I prepay on my student loans?" The answer to that is - it depends. While each situation is unique, in general you should pay off high interest rate consumer debt first, such as credit cards, auto loans, and other consumer debt, including private student loans. It may also make sense to be sure you are getting any retirement match at work and that your emergency fund is funded. After that it probably makes sense to put extra money towards your student loan.

Other financial planners would disagree with me and say a borrower should never prepay federal loans because student loans are generally low interest and you can deduct that interest from your taxes. However, if you have a time of life when you can't make payments (such as during an illness or period of unemployment) then those benefits (low, tax-deductible interest) won't help much. Sure, you can put the loans on deferment or forbearance, but then interest is adding on to most of your loans, which could negate any previous benefits.

I am a big fan of getting debt, including student loan debt, paid off as quickly as possible.

10. WHAT REPAYMENT OPTIONS
ARE AVAILABLE?

Once a student graduates, drops below half-time status or drops out of school their loan enters the repayment phase. Most loans have a six-month grace period (nine months for Perkins) where no payments have to be made. Be aware, though, that interest will be accruing on any unsubsidized loans.

Traditional Payment Plans

Standard: The Standard plan is a 10-year level repayment plan, with a minimum monthly payment of $50. Borrowers will pay less interest on the Standard plan, but they will also have the highest payment. The Standard plan is the default plan unless another repayment plan is selected. Your monthly payment is determined by the total debt, the interest rate, and the total length of repayment (no longer than ten years).

Standard Graduated: This plan starts out with a low payment, then every two years the payments step up. It is still paid off in 10 years, but with higher interest than the Standard plan. Payments will never be less than the interest that is accruing. The monthly payment is determined by total debt, the interest rate, and the total length of repayment (no longer than ten years).

Extended: This plan is a 25-year level repayment plan. You must have $30,000 or more in loans to qualify for this plan. Because the borrower is stretching the repayment out for 25 years payments will be lower, but more interest will be paid. The monthly payment is determined by total debt, the interest rate, and the total length of repayment (no longer than 25 years).

Extended Graduated: This is a plan that is only available for Direct Consolidation loans. The length of repayment depends on the total amount of debt (combined Consolidation loans and non-consolidated loans). The payment starts out low and increases every two years. Payments will never be less than the interest that is accruing. The monthly payment is determined by total debt, the interest rate, and the total length of repayment (no longer than 30 years).

The payment term is determined by the amount of debt:

At least	Less than	Repayment Period
	$7,500	10 years
$7,500	$10,000	12 years
$10,000	$20,000	15 years
$20,000	$40,000	20 years
$40,000	$60,000	25 years
$60,000		30 years

To illustrate these repayment plans, let's imagine a borrower, Alex, has $35,000 in subsidized loans with a 4.7% interest rate. Here is how much the payment would be on each of the traditional plans:

Plan	Monthly Payment	Total Interest Paid	Total Paid
Standard	$366	$8,934	$43,934
Standard Graduated	$206 - $619	$11,212	$46,212
Extended	$199	$24,561	$59,561
Extended Graduated	$137 - $332	$30,102	$65,102

Income-Driven Repayment Plans (IDR)

There are several repayment plans that are based on income and a person's family size. All of these plans utilize a number called discretionary income, which is Adjusted Gross Income (AGI) minus 150% of the poverty level. For all 48 contiguous states the poverty level is the same, while it is higher in Hawaii and Alaska.

Let's say our borrower, Alex, makes $35,000 (AGI) and that 150% of the poverty level for his family size is $25,000. Alex would have Discretionary Income of $10,000 ($35,000 - $25,000). We will use Alex's Discretionary Income of $10,000 in each example.

Income-Based Repayment (IBR): To qualify for the IBR plan you need a partial financial hardship, which is when your payment under the Standard plan would exceed 15 percent of your Discretionary Income as defined above.

Payments are 15% of your Discretionary Income. In the example with Alex his payment would be $1,500 per year, or $125 per month. Payments are recalculated annually, however, the payment will never be higher than the Standard payment, and any remaining amount is forgiven after 25 years. However, whatever amount is forgiven is taxable as income in that year.

Income-Based Repayment (IBR) for new borrowers: If a borrower is a new borrower after July 1, 2014 and they have a partial financial hardship they qualify for New IBR. Everything is the same as IBR except you pay 10% of your discretionary income, which would make Alex's payment $1,000 a year, or $83 per month. Forgiveness happens after 20 years instead of 25, however the forgiven amount is taxable as income. The payment is recalculated annually but the payment will never be higher than the Standard payment.

Pay As You Earn (PAYE): To qualify for the PAYE plan you need a partial financial hardship, which is when your payment under the Standard plan would exceed 10 percent of your Discretionary Income as defined above. PAYE is identical to new IBR, except that the requirements for utilizing it are more stringent. You have to be a new borrower after Oct 1, 2007 and received at least one disbursement after October 1, 2011. The payment will never be higher than the Standard repayment amount.

Revised Pay As You Earn (REPAYE): Any borrower is eligible for the REPAYE plan. Payments are 10% of a borrower's Discretionary Income with no limit to how high the payment can go. The payment is recalculated annually. Forgiveness takes place after 20 years for undergraduate loans only and 25 years if any graduate loans are being repaid. The forgiven amount is taxable as income.

Income-Contingent Repayment (ICR): The ICR plan is generally 20% of your Discretionary Income, but instead of using 150% of the poverty level 100% is used, which would make Alex's Discretionary Income $18,000 ($35,000 - $17,000), and his payment $3,600 per year, or $300 per month. Repayment can go up to 25 years, with any remaining amount forgiven and taxable as income. ICR is the only income-driven plan that can be utilized by Parent PLUS borrowers, but they must consolidate their Parent PLUS loans into a Consolidation loan first.

The reality is that most of these income-based plans are probably going away. The ICR plan is extremely unpopular. The original IBR plan has been replaced by the new IBR plan and the PAYE plan is far too restrictive, so it is being replaced by the New IBR plan. I can foresee the day when only the new IBR plan and REPAYE remain.

If Alex's AGI is $35,000 and he is married with 2 children his payments would be:

Plan	Monthly Payment	Length of repayment	Total repaid	Projected Loan Forgiveness
IBR (15%)	$0 - $366/month	25 years	$56,080	$18,026
New IBR & PAYE (10%)	$0 - $255/month	20 years	$22,901	$44,999
REPAYE (10%)	$0 - $398/month	20 or 25 years	$43,170	$21,956
ICR (20%)	$173 - $311/month	25 years	$51,845	$0

NOTE: The calculator assumes that Alex's income will go up 5% per year, which is why payments go up over time.

It would seem to make sense for Alex to repay using New IBR or PAYE, right? Those plans have the lowest payment, the least amount repaid, and the largest projected loan forgiveness. However, remember that the amount forgiven is taxable as income. If Alex is in a 15% tax bracket he will pay approximately $6,750 in taxes, which does not eliminate New IBR or PAYE as the best choice, but it is something to consider.

Whether or not you can utilize a repayment plan depends on the type of loan you have:

- Direct Subsidized, Direct Unsubsidized, Graduate PLUS
  - All repayment plans except Extended Graduated
- Direct Consolidation Loan
  - All repayment plans including Extended Graduated
- Parent PLUS
  - Standard, Standard Graduated, Extended
- Consolidation loans for Parent PLUS loans
  - Standard, Standard Graduated, Extended, ICR

11. CAN I SWITCH REPAYMENT PLANS?

Yes, you can switch repayment plans as often as you want, for free. If you cannot change it directly on the servicer's website you can call the servicer and switch it. Your servicer may limit how often you can change plans, for example they might say you can only change plans monthly, but there will never be a charge to switch plans.

STUDENT LOAN STORY

Camille[3] graduated with two associate's degrees, a bachelor's degree, and a bill for a total of $54,740. Her current balance is $72,573.

"My husband and I were both first generation college students. We were trying to finish college no matter what it took, and nobody before us ever had student loans. We did entrance counseling but that just reinforced that we would have to pay them back. I don't think we truly had any idea what we were doing to ourselves.

"Our student loans kept us from buying a house all these years and having our loans on deferment lost us a USDA loan.

"We can't even afford the interest on our student loans. There's no hope of paying the principal. We're basically holding out for the forgiveness after 25 years deal while paying $100 a month of interest.

"It's horrible and heartbreaking.

"I have so many regrets. One of the biggest regrets is that there is no possibility of me being a stay-at-home mom, ever. I am truly a slave to my paycheck."

---

[3] Name has been changed

12. HOW DO INCOME-BASED REPAYMENT PLANS WORK IF MY INCOME IS BELOW THE POVERTY LEVEL?

In the example shared above for Alex, you can see that under some repayment plans his payment would be $0 to start out. That is not a mistake - his payment is $0 and it is considered an on-time, made-in-full payment.

But that, of course, is not the full story. Interest is still accruing during this time, so what happens to the interest?

Under the REPAYE, PAYE and IBR plans if your payment doesn't cover the interest the government will pay the unpaid interest on your subsidized loans for up to three consecutive years. Under the REPAYE plan half the unpaid interest on subsidized loans will be paid after the three years and half the unpaid interest will be paid on unsubsidized loans during all periods. Any interest not covered will accrue and be added to your loan.

For example, if Alex's payment is $0 a month, but his loan is accumulating $50 of interest per month on his subsidized loans and $50 of interest per month on his unsubsidized loans the interest would work like this:

PAYE, IBR:

Interest	Time Period	Amount added to loan per month	Amount added to loan after 20 years
$50 subsidized	Years 1-3	$0	$0
$50 subsidized	Years 4 - termination of loan	$50	$10,200
$50 unsubsidized	Years 1 – termination of loan	$50	$12,000

REPAYE:

Interest	Time Period	Amount added to loan per month	Amount added to loan after 20 years
$50 subsidized	Years 1-3	$0	$0
$50 subsidized	Years 4 - termination of loan	$25	$5,100
$50 unsubsidized	Years 1 – termination of loan	$25	$6,000

If Alex's payment remains at $0 for 20 years under the IBR or PAYE plan he will have a total of $22,200 in interest added to his loan, which will increase the amount of forgiveness he will receive, all of which is taxable as income to Alex. If Alex is in a 15% tax bracket he will owe taxes of $3,330 on the accumulated interest.

If Alex's payment remains at $0 for 20 years under the REPAYE plan he will have a total of $11,100 in interest added to his loan, which will again increase the amount of taxable forgiveness, but at a far lower amount than IBR or PAYE. If Alex is in a 15% tax bracket he will owe taxes of $1,665 on the interest that has accumulated.

Can you see how critical it is to select the right repayment plan?

There is a lot of information to consider!

13. I HAVE HEARD I CAN REDUCE MY PAYMENTS IF I FILE MARRIED FILING SEPARATELY (MFS). IS THAT TRUE?

For most repayment plans the answer is no, your payments won't be lower if you file MFS. The exceptions to that are IBR, new IBR, PAYE and ICR. On these plans if you file MFS only the borrower's income will count towards the AGI (Adjusted Gross Income), thereby creating a lower payment and higher amount forgiven since not all income is included. This scenario typically works best when one spouse has a high loan balance and has low income. Remember, though, that under current law, anything forgiven is taxable as income.

As filing MFS causes the loss of some benefits, if you think this is a strategy you may benefit from, talk with a tax advisor.

STUDENT LOAN STORY

Students who drop out of college without a degree face higher unemployment rates, lower lifetime earnings, and higher unemployment rates than their peers who graduate[vii].

DeAngelo Bowie[viii] is one of those students. Bowie enrolled as a first generation college student at Georgia State University in order to become a history teacher. Facing financial pressure and lacking the necessary study skills to succeed in college, he dropped out of school with $12,000 in student loan debt. Trying to pay off his debt he took a job at a warehouse but was unable to make any progress on his loans.

When he tried to re-apply to school and get loans he learned that his loans were in default and had been sold to a collection agency, so he was ineligible for more student loans.

Bowie faces a tough situation that thousands of other borrowers face. Students like Bowie need help to avoid these types of problems. His relatively small amount of debt is keeping him from living his dreams and stuck him in a low-paying job. Having more direct intervention from the University, his loan servicer or others could have easily prevented this situation.

14. WHAT IS THE BEST REPAYMENT PLAN?

There is no one *best* plan. A number of factors go into the answer to this question, and it is a good idea to get help from someone who is knowledgeable about student loans.

However, there are several factors to consider.

Paying off your loan as fast as possible is generally a good idea, but paying off high interest, non-deductible debt, such as credit cards, auto loans and private student loans should be a higher priority. You will still pay the minimum on your student loans, but it may be worth stretching your payments out for a longer period of time to focus on paying down other debt.

It is also important to consider your budget and how much you can afford.

If you are thinking about an income-based plan it is important to remember that taxes will likely be due at the end of the repayment term on any amount that is forgiven.

If you are planning on working in the public sector or for a non-profit you may want to consider utilizing the Public Service Loan Forgiveness (PSLF) program. See the Question 19 for more information about PSLF.

15. WHAT IS LOAN CONSOLIDATION AND WHEN SHOULD I CONSIDER IT?

Loan consolidation is taking all or some of your existing loans and combining them into a single loan to get a single interest rate and a single payment.

In-school consolidation is no longer an option, nor is spouse loan consolidation (combining the loans of a married couple). You can also only consolidate your loans one time.

There are several private student loan companies that market aggressively to convince you that you should refinance your federal student loans into a private student loan. There are few scenarios where that makes sense. See Question 16 for more details.

The reality is that consolidation doesn't offer many benefits anymore. In fact, often a borrower will find that their interest rate is slightly higher than what they were paying before. All of your loans are likely held by one student loan servicer, so you will only have one payment anyway.

If you happen to have loans with multiple servicers consolidation will make tracking and making payments easier.

If you are going to consolidate there are several things you should know.

1. Don't consolidate during your 6-month grace period. If you do you are waiving your grace period and repayment will start immediately. You want to wait until month five to start the

consolidation process, or be sure to indicate on the consolidation application to delay consolidation until your grace period ends.

2. If you are working on the Public Service Loan Forgiveness Program (see Question 19) you cannot consolidate or the 120 payment clock will start back over.

3. If you are utilizing an income-driven repayment plan consolidating your loans will restart the clock for payments made toward forgiveness.

4. FFEL loans (not Direct loans) are ineligible for Public Service Loan Forgiveness and the repayment plans ICR, New IBR, PAYE or REPAYE. FFEL loans need to be consolidated with a Direct Consolidation Loan to take advantage of any of those programs.

5. You can choose which loans to consolidate - you don't have to include all of them if you do not want to. One strategy that is recommended is to leave one loan out of consolidation so you have the option to re-consolidate later if you need to.

You can apply for a consolidation loan at StudentLoans.gov.

16. DOES IT EVER MAKE SENSE TO REFINANCE FEDERAL LOANS INTO A PRIVATE LOAN?

For most situations, the answer is no. The main reason you should not do this is because you lose government provided benefits such as deferment, forbearance, flexible payment plans, Public Service Loan Forgiveness and fixed interest rates. If you plan to take advantage of any of these benefits do not refinance your loans to a private loan.

There might be a few circumstances where it could make sense:

- You do not plan to utilize any of the benefits of government loans.

- You have a high income and high student loan debt, with the majority of your debt being higher interest PLUS loans or unsubsidized loans.

- You can get a fixed interest rate that is lower than your current rate.

17. IS STUDENT LOAN INTEREST TAX DEDUCTIBLE?

For most borrowers the answer is yes, up to $2,500 per year. In fact, it is the best type of deduction (above the line, which means it reduces your income dollar-for-dollar, resulting in less of your income being taxed).

Check with your tax preparer to see if interest will be deductible for you.

STUDENT LOAN STORY

Jason Yoder[ix] was a graduate student in Organic Chemistry at Illinois State University. Weighed down with more than $100,000 in student loan debt and unable to find a job, Jason took his own life.

Unfortunately, Jason's story is not an uncommon one. There are far too many stories on the internet about people either committing suicide or planning to because of their student loan debt.

If you or someone you know is contemplating suicide please, get help. Call the National Suicide Prevention Lifeline at 1-800-273-8255.

18. CAN I MAKE MY PAYMENT WITH A CREDIT CARD?

The general answer to this question is no. Most student loan servicers only allow payment from a checking or savings account. If you do find a 3rd-party provider or servicer who allows it, they will likely charge a fee.

However, if you are struggling to make payments on your student loans, transferring the payment to a credit card isn't going to fix anything. Credit cards typically have much higher interest rates than student loans, so your payment will be much higher on a credit card.

The only time it might make sense to pay your student loan with a credit card would be if you can pay your credit card balance in full and you are earning rewards. However, if the servicer charges an additional fee to pay with a credit card it will probably outweigh the reward you are getting.

19. WHAT IS PUBLIC SERVICE LOAN FORGIVENESS (PSLF)?

Public Service Loan Forgiveness (PSLF) was established to encourage graduates to work for the government or the public sector. The idea is that a person makes less working in the public sector than they would working in the private sector. While this may or may not be true, it is a benefit that is available.

The requirements are that you need to make qualifying payments with qualifying loans, under a qualifying repayment plan while working full-time for a qualifying employer. That's a lot of qualifying! Let's break each one down:

- Qualifying payments
    - o Payments need to be for the full amount due and paid within 15 dates of the due date to count.
    - o Payments made in school, during the grace period or while in deferment or forbearance do not count, nor do extra payments.
    - o Payments do not need to be consecutive - that means the borrower can make 100 qualifying payments, then work for a for-profit organization for 2 years, then return to a qualifying employer and make 20 more payments.
    - o Only payments made after October 1, 2007 are eligible.
- Qualifying loans
    - o Only Direct loans that are not in default are eligible. If a borrower has FFEL loans those loans need to be

consolidated into a Direct Consolidation loan to be eligible.

- o Parent PLUS loans do qualify, but the borrower (not the student) has to work for a qualifying employer. In order to take advantage of PSLF a borrower would need to consolidate the loans and pay using the only income-driven repayment plan available for Parent PLUS loans – Income-Contingent Repayment (ICR).

- Qualifying repayment plan
    - o Qualifying repayment plans include all the income-driven plans. Be sure you are not in a graduated repayment plan or extended repayment plan as these do not qualify!

- Qualifying employer
    - o Qualifying employers include any government organizations (including federal, state, local, or tribal); or a non-profit organization (501(c)(3)), or with the Peace Corps or AmeriCorps. This generally includes:
        - Military service
        - Public safety
        - Public education
        - Public health
        - Public libraries
        - First responders
        - Social workers
    - o It does not matter what job the borrower has, just who the employer is.
    - o The job must be full time, which is considered 30-hours per week or more.

o   Organizations excluded include labor unions, partisan political organizations, and proselytizing activities.

o   If the borrower is a teacher with a summer break their contract needs to be for at least 8 months, they need to average 30 hours per week (except during the break), and the employer needs to consider you to be employed full-time, including during the summer.

o   The borrower does not need to stay with the same employer the full time.

o   You must still be employed by a qualifying employer until forgiveness is complete.

The program is all or nothing. If you make 119 qualifying payments and then switch to a private sector job nothing is forgiven.

To start the process, you need to fill out the Public Service Loan Forgiveness Employment Certification Form at studentaid.ed.gov (just search for the form name). This form also needs to be re-submitted each year *or* anytime you switch employers. Once the form has been verified you will receive a letter telling you how many payments have been made towards the 120 payments. Keep copies of all of these letters, along with copies of the Certification Form.

You have to apply for forgiveness after the 120 payments - it is not automatic.

There is currently no limit to the amount you can have forgiven, and the forgiven amount is not taxable.

If you have already started making qualified payments on a loan DO NOT consolidate that loan as it will start the clock back over for your 120 payments.

The first question I am asked when discussing PSLF it whether or not the program will be there in the future. My answer is that I don't think it will be there in the same form it is now. President Obama wanted the amount forgiven reduced to about $57,000, and President Trump has recommended the program be eliminated. Congress established the program and Congress can take it away or revise it. My guess is that if changes are made those who are currently in school or in repayment will be grandfathered in under the current rules, but there is no guarantee of that.

As you can imagine, with unlimited tax-free forgiveness there have been abuses of the system. Why not take out all you can, pay for your vehicle, computer, study abroad, etc., then just have it all written off after ten years? I know people who have done this very thing. For this reason, I would support legislation to limit the amount that can be forgiven.

STUDENT LOAN STORY

Steven and Kim[4] finished their undergraduate degrees with very little debt. Steven paid for his education using student loans for tuition coupled with a part-time job for other expenses.

"I decided to transfer to a school closer to home so I could live at home while attending classes. My expenses dropped, and I had a full-time job. I paid tuition out of pocket, and I even started making payments on my small student loan debt. Then I lost my job. At this point, Kim and I had been married a few years and were about two months from the birth of our first baby. I started working for a friend and took out student loans to cover tuition and books. For my final two semesters, my school schedule became so crazy that it negated my ability to work and attend classes. I quit my job and took out student loans to pay for school and lifestyle. By the time I graduated, I had around $20,000 in student loan debt.

"My goal was to teach in higher education, so I needed graduate school. We moved to Texas to go to school about three weeks after the birth of our second child. I had a teaching assistantship which included full tuition, but even with these benefits, our total income was well below the poverty line. We applied for public assistance for healthcare and student loans to cover rent.

"After a couple years, and the addition of another child, our vehicle's engine died. We decided to use a student loan to purchase a used car. We graduated a couple years later, after 6.5 years in graduate school, partly motivated at the end by the lifetime lending limit for

---

[4] Names have been changed

student loans of $138,000.

"We had the cheapest apartment available for a family and we lived in pretty awful conditions for five years. We relied on government benefits and the kindness of family and friends for the six years it took to get my first teaching job, and still racked up $140,000 in student loan debt.

"Really, the best way to overcome the student loan problem in our case would have been to find a job in the field, possibly through government, then slowly work towards the Ph.D. so I could teach. Since I was impatient, student loans provided the opportunity on the classic receive now, pay later model. I now have the benefit of my graduate education, but make monthly payments adjusted to my income until I'm 60. It's working out, but it would have been nice to avoid the debt."

Steven and Kim are enrolled in the Income Based Repayment program, and their student loan debt will end up costing them well over $200,000.

20. WHAT IS TEACHER LOAN FORGIVENESS?

K-12 teachers who teach full-time for five full academic years in a low-income school can have up to $17,500 of their subsidized and unsubsidized loans forgiven. If you teach math or science at the secondary school level or special education at the elementary or secondary level you can receive forgiveness of up to $17,500, while other teachers in a low-income school can receive forgiveness of up to $5,000.

Borrowers cannot count the five years that are used for Teacher Forgiveness towards Public Service Loan Forgiveness (PSLF - see question 19 for more details). You start the 120 payments towards that program after completing the Teacher Forgiveness program.

21. ARE THERE OTHER OPPORTUNITIES FOR MY LOAN TO BE FORGIVEN, CANCELLED OR DISCHARGED?

If your school closes while you are going to school, you may qualify to have some or all of your student loans forgiven.

If a debtor becomes permanently and totally disabled or they die federal student loans are forgiven and, under current law, the forgiven balance is not taxable. Student loans are not passed on to a spouse or other family members when the borrower passes away.

Parent PLUS loans can be eliminated if the borrower (typically a parent) becomes disabled or dies, but if the parents took the loan out together both would need to be disabled or die for the loan to be discharged. If the student for whom the loan the taken out passes away Parent PLUS loans can be forgiven.

STUDENT LOAN STORY

Jennifer graduated with almost $80,000 in student loan debt. Her payments were high, so a private lender convinced her to refinance her loans. Unfortunately, her new interest rate is variable, and she now has an interest rate of 11% and a payment of almost $900 per month.

Jennifer works for a non-profit company, and would have qualified for a very low payment under an income-driven repayment plan, and she would have qualified for Public Service Loan Forgiveness (PSLF) after 10 years of payments.

Unfortunately, Jennifer has no recourse. She cannot consolidate her loans back into a federal loan. Because of an unscrupulous lender who only had their best interests at heart, Jennifer has lost all the benefits she would have received with a federal loan.

22. CAN STUDENT LOANS BE DISCHARGED IN BANKRUPTCY?

Maybe. Sometimes. Don't count on it. Historically student loans have been like child support and tax debt - not dischargeable in bankruptcy. However, because of the Bankruptcy Abuse Prevention and Consumer Protection Act of 2005 if it can be proven that student loans cause "undue hardship" then it is possible to discharge some or all of them.

Undue hardship is left up to the bankruptcy judge to determine, but most judges utilize a similar standard:

- The debtor has made a good faith effort to repay their loan.
- The debtor is expected to have long-standing circumstances that will prevent them from making payments. This long-standing circumstance does not include total disability - see Question 21 for more information on disability discharge.

Private student loans enjoy the same bankruptcy protection as federal student loans, which speaks to the power of the student loan lobbying efforts.

23. WHAT SHOULD I DO IF I AM HAVING TROUBLE MAKING MY PAYMENTS?

"Not paying back your student loans is one of the worst decisions you can make next to marrying the wrong person. They never go away and they're going to haunt you forever!" –Paul Lerma, El Paso Community College

It is important that you avoid getting behind on your payments.

If you are having trouble making payments, or know that you are going to due to a change in income, you should take immediate steps. First, consider an income-based repayment plan, even for a little while. If your income has gone down this could reduce your payment as low as $0 per month.

The next strategy to consider is deferment. When your loans are in deferment you do not have to make any payments. Deferment is granted by a lender under special circumstances, such as financial hardship, job loss or military deployment. Your subsidized loans do not accrue any interest during deferment; however, all unsubsidized loans do accrue interest.

If you don't qualify for deferment, then consider forbearance. During forbearance you don't have to make any payments, but all of your loans accrue interest.

Because at least some of your loans are accruing interest during deferment or forbearance, these strategies should be utilized sparingly for a short period of time, and if you can afford to pay the interest rather than allowing it to accrue, you will be better off. For both deferment and forbearance any interest that accrues will be capitalized when you go back into repayment. This means that the interest that accrues will be added to the principal, which will make your loan balance and payments go up.

Lending institutions, such as banks and credit unions, may look on deferment and forbearance as negative and they may assume that you cannot pay your bills.

I recommend you consider extreme measures to pay off your debt. For example, when my wife and I wanted to pay off some debt we chose to move to Korea to teach English for a year. We applied all extra money to our debt, which allowed us to clear up almost all of our consumer and student loan debts.

STUDENT LOAN STORY

How about an inspiring student loan story? Kody and Bethany Morris[x] finished graduate school with just over $130,000 in debt between them.

Determined to pay off their debt as quickly as possible, both worked full-time and Kody picked up a second full-time job while Bethany picked up a second part-time job. They created a tight budget and put every extra dollar towards their debt, including cash gifts received. They created a visual tracker where they marked off every $1,000 they paid off.

Because of their diligence and dedication to the goal, Kody and Bethany paid off their debt in just five years, saving tens of thousands of dollars in interest.

24. WHAT IS STUDENT LOAN DEFAULT?

Student loans are in default after 270 days, or 9 months, of no payments. You do not want to be in default on your student loans! I want to stress the importance of taking other steps (see Question 23 for more details) instead of defaulting.

A borrower who defaults on their loans faces the following consequences:

- Collection fees of up to 25% (this means that if Alex defaults on his $35,000 in loans and has a 25% collection fee of $8,750, his new balance will be $43,750)
- Aggressive debt collection practices
- Wage garnishment (part of your wages will be taken) without a court order
- Seizure of tax refunds
- Seizure of part of your Social Security wages
- Damaged credit rating
- Ineligibility for future financial aid

Again, **avoid default**. Technically you can send a payment in before the 270 days are up and the clock starts back over, but I would caution you to be careful playing that game as the law could change at any time. If you are already in default, see the Question 25.

25. ARE THERE OPPORTUNITIES TO GET OUT OF DEFAULT?

Yes, you can get out of default utilizing one of three methods:

1. Start making on-time payments and pay the full amount back. This isn't a formal program to get out of default, it is simply paying back the full amount. It is possible to settle for a lower amount, but you would need a large, lump-sum to offer.

2. Consolidation:
   a. Consolidation is a one-time deal to get out of default.
   b. A collection fee of no more than 18.5% will be added to your loan.
   c. You can only re-consolidate if you have a consolidation loan and another loan to combine with your current consolidation loan. If you consolidated all your loans after school, for example, then went into default, you would not be able to use a consolidation loan to get out of default.
   d. If your wages are being garnished, you cannot consolidate your loans. You can request to have the garnishment lifted if you would like to take this route.
   e. If you make three full on-time payments you can utilize any repayment plan, if you do not make three full on-time payments you need to agree to repay your loan using IBR, PAYE, REPAYE or ICR.
   f. After getting out of default the record of the default remains on your credit report for seven years.

3. Rehabilitation:
   a. Rehabilitation is also a one-time deal to get out of default.

b. A collection fee of no more than 16% will be added to your loan.

c. You will pay approximately 15% of your annual discretionary income as defined for the IBR plan.

d. You must make nine out of ten payments on-time.

e. After the nine payments are complete the default will be removed from your credit report, but the record of late payments will remain for seven years.

If you are in default call your servicer right away to discuss options. After getting out of default most benefits, such as the ability to get future financial aid, are restored.

26. ADVICE FROM OTHER BORROWERS

I have talked to many student loan borrowers over the years and I like to ask them what they would tell other students and borrowers. The most common regret is taking on so much in student loans instead of taking out the minimum needed. Here are some of their other thoughts:

- Be cautious about returning to school on loans for a graduate degree or certificate.
- Student loan debt may make it difficult to buy a home.
- By taking out too much in loans we paid huge monthly payments that basically only covered the interest - try to limit the amount you take out to just tuition.
- Don't take out private loans.
- During school be aware of how much repayment is going to be.
- Pay the interest on unsubsidized loans while you are going to school.
- Discuss your student loan debt with your fiancé before you get married.
- Try to live as cheaply as possible – don't live in luxury student housing and cook most of your meals at home.
- Work while you go to school to pay for books, food, and entertainment.
- Go to a community college for the first two years.
- Limit your student loans to only subsidized loans.
- Don't use deferment or forbearance if it can be avoided.
- Don't ever go into default on your loans.
- Pay back your loans as quickly as possible after graduation.

- When consolidating leave one loan out – that way you can consolidate again if needed.
- Review your student loans and the payment plan you are on anytime you change jobs, have a change in pay, change your relationship status or change your family size. In addition, it is a good idea to do a review of your loans each year to track your progress.
- Remember to file the annual documentation each year for the income-driven repayment plans and the Employment Certification Form for PSLF each year (or when you change employers).

27. WHO SHOULD I CONTACT IF I NEED HELP?

Based on everything you have read so far, is it surprising that borrowers find student loans confusing? You want to make sure you are in the right repayment plan where you will pay off your loans quickly, while staying within your budget and minimizing the tax consequences. There are forms to navigate each year with Income-Driven plans and Public Service Loan Forgiveness. On top of all of that, the laws keep changing.

If you feel like you need some help with your student loans, there are several resources available to help you:

1. Your loan servicer. You can always call them or e-mail questions. You may or may not get accurate information from them. I have heard stories of very wrong information being given by the servicer, but there is no recourse for the borrower if they follow incorrect information.

2. There are some great websites that can be very helpful including:
   a. studentaid.ed.gov
   b. nslds.ed.gov
   c. loanconsolidation.ed.gov
   d. studentloans.gov

3. If you have a high loan balance or are planning to utilize income-driven plans or Public Service Loan Forgiveness or you just want to make sure you are on the right path I recommend you get advice from a competent professional, whether it is me or someone else. These services are not free, but a competent professional can help you avoid some very expensive mistakes.

Wouldn't you feel better, for example, knowing you have everything in place for Public Service Loan Forgiveness than to get to year 10 and realize that you had one portion incorrect and you have to start the 10-year clock back over? If you want help, visit my website at https://ryanhlaw.com.

28. CHANGES NEEDED IN THE STUDENT LOAN INDUSTRY

While I mainly want this book to be about your loans and how to get them paid off as quickly as possible, there are several things that I think need to change in the industry. Here is my list of 10 items I think need to change:

1. Make all students independent so they do not have to use their parent's information for the FAFSA.

2. Eliminate all origination fees. The government makes enough money from the interest.

3. Borrowers should have an annual visit with a person while they are in school to review their balance and payments, and again at graduation.

4. Annual award letter should list the borrower's total debt as well as the monthly payment on a Standard 10-year plan.

5. Allow consolidation more than one time, except to get out of default.

6. Limit Public Service Loan Forgiveness to reduce abuse.

7. All First Responders and Military members should get tax-free forgiveness after five years of service, up to a maximum amount.

8. Reduce or eliminate collection fees one time when student successfully rehabilitates their defaulted loan.

9. At a minimum, eliminate IBR, ICR, and PAYE; and open REPAYE for Parent PLUS loans.

10. Each state should have a student loan advocate or ombudsman to help borrowers understand their rights and responsibilities like Virginia, Washington, Illinois, Connecticut and other states have done.

STUDENT LOAN STORY

Ben[5] financed his education with loans, then upon graduation he consolidated his loans. His interest rate was high – over 10%, which made his payments higher than expected. When rates dropped he tried to consolidate again to take advantage of lower rates, but he was told that since he already consolidated once he couldn't do it again. Ben petitioned his servicer and even his Congressmen, but to no avail.

Burdened by the large payments, Ben finally refinanced his loans with a private student loan company, which dropped his interest rates down to about 4%. He realizes that by refinancing with a private company he lost the benefits of government loans, but his payment was unmanageable.

How does Ben feel about the student loan industry?

"It seemed at the time that the government was trying to help students through their guaranteed student loan programs, but in hindsight and through painful experience, I now see it as a trap. That may not have been the original intent of the government, but it was the effect. Things were set up in favor of the banks and loan servicing companies who were basically preying on naïve students and were emboldened by the government guarantees."

---

[5] Name has been changed

29. FINAL THOUGHTS

Yes, student loans are confusing. Yes, Congress changes the rules, making it harder to follow what is happening.

However, you can get your student loans paid off. Re-read the Morris' story again. I would encourage you to follow their advice - take on extra work, trim your budget as much as possible, create a visual tracker showing your progress and amount left, stay motivated and throw every extra dollar at your debt. Pay off higher interest, non-deductible debt first, and then crush your student loan debt as fast as possible.

None of us know what the future holds. If one of the Morris' becomes disabled or they are unable to work for a period of time they don't have to worry about their student loan debt. **That is freedom.**

If you are a student now or you are planning to go to school soon, do everything you can to keep your loan balances as low as possible.

Thank you for reading. I welcome your comments and stories. You can connect with me and keep up with what is happening with student loans at my website – https://ryanhlaw.com.

ACKNOWLEDGMENTS

I would like to thank my wife, Traci, and our children for their support and patience as I worked on this project. I would also like to thank all my professors and colleagues at Utah State, Iowa State, Texas Tech, University of Missouri, and Utah Valley University.

ABOUT THE AUTHOR

Ryan H. Law is a CERTIFIED FINANCIAL PLANNER™ (CFP®) and an Accredited Financial Counselor (AFC®). He has a Bachelor's degree in Family Finance from Utah State University and a Master's degree in Personal Financial Planning from Texas Tech University. Ryan has been teaching college courses in personal financial planning for nine years – first at the University of Missouri and currently at Utah Valley University. He is a co-editor of the book *Financial Counseling*.

Ryan lives in Utah with his wife and children.

NOTES AND REFERENCES

[i] Grant, H.J. (1942). *Gospel standards: Selections from the sermons and writings of Heber J. Grant.* Salt Lake City, UT: Improvement Era, pp. 111

[ii] Klepfer, K., Ashton, B., Bradley, D., Fernandez, C., Wartel, M., Webster, J. (2018 June) *Student financial wellness survey report.* Retrieved from https://www.trelliscompany.org/student-finance-survey/

[iii] For information on the best 529 plans, read Morningstar's article about 529 plans at http://www.morningstar.com/articles/867032/the-best-529-plans.html

[iv] Perna, L.W. (2010). Understanding the working college student, *Academe.* Retrieved from https://www.aaup.org/article/understanding-working-college-student#.Ww862UgvyUl

[v] Mitchell, J. (2018, May 25). Mike Meru has $1 million in student loans. How did that happen? *The Wall Street Journal.* Retrieved from https://www.wsj.com/articles/mike-meru-has-1-million-in-student-loans-how-did-that-happen-1527252975

[vi] Collinge, A. (2010). *The student loan scam: The most oppressive debt in U.S. history and how we can fight back.* Boston, MA: Beacon Press, pp. xi

[vii] Nguyen, M. (2012, Feb 23). Degreeless in debt: What happens to borrowers who drop out. *American Institutes for Research.* Retrieved from https://www.air.org/edsector-archives/publications/degreeless-debt-what-happens-borrowers-who-drop-out

[viii] Kolodner, M. & Butrymowicz, S. (2017, Aug 24). How students with school debt but no degree get stuck in 'purgatory.' PBS News Hour. Retrieved from https://www.pbs.org/newshour/education/students-school-debt-no-degree-get-stuck-pugatory

[ix] Johannsen, C.C. (2012, Sept 1). The ones we've lost: The student loan debt suicides. *Huffington Post.* Retrieved from https://www.huffingtonpost.com/entry/student-loan-debt-suicides_b_1638972.html

[x] Jesuweit, A. (2017, Jun 23). How this family crushed $130,000 in student loans in just 5 years. *Forbes.* Retrieved from https://www.forbes.com/sites/andrewjosuweit/2017/06/23/how-this-family-crushed-130000-in-student-loans-in-just-5-years/#7a803e5865d8

Made in the USA
San Bernardino, CA
14 June 2019